The origins of Jarrow the monastery, the sl_... Ecgfrith's minster

Ian Wood

Bede's World Studies: 1

Frontispiece. Dedication stone from St Paul's church, Jarrow 23 April 685.

The origins of Jarrow: the monastery, the slake and Ecgfrith's minster

Among the many notable things about Jarrow is the dedication stone of its original church. Its inscription reads:

> *The Dedication of the basilica of St Paul on the 9th day before the Kalends of May in the fifteenth year of king Ecgfrith, and in the 4th of abbot Ceolfrid, founder, by the guidance of God, of the same Church.*[1]

It is a remarkable survival: there is nothing else quite like it for Anglo-Saxon England. It tells us, quite clearly, that the monastery was founded by Ceolfrid, and it gives a date for the dedication of the church in terms of his abbacy and of the regnal years of king Ecgfrith. It was the fifteenth year of the king's reign, and the fourth year of Ceolfrid's abbacy. The fifteenth year of Ecgfrith would have begun in February 685, and since the monastery at Jarrow is said elsewhere to have been founded in 681/2, concurrent dating to Ceolfrid's fourth year must mean that the dedication took place in 685.[2]

Despite this clarity there are problems, for the stone, with its emphasis on Ceolfrid as founder, gives a very different impression from that given by Bede in the account of the foundation of Jarrow in his *History of the Abbots*.

> *King Ecgfrith was thoroughly pleased with the good qualities, hard work and devotion of the venerable Benedict [Biscop]. He took pains to increase the land which he had given to him to build the monastery [Wearmouth], because he saw that he had given well and fruitfully, and granted him ownership of a further*

3

forty hides [i.e. the estate at Jarrow]. Benedict sent some monks there, a good seventeen in number, with the priest Ceolfrid over them as their abbot, and a year later, by the decision and indeed by the command of the said king Ecgfrith, [he, Benedict] built the monastery of the blessed apostle Paul, on the basis that a single peaceful harmony and the same friendship and grace should be maintained in each of the two places in perpetuity, so that just as (to use an illustration) the body cannot be torn from the head, through which it breathes, and the head cannot forget about the body, without which it does not live, so no man should try by any attempt to split these monasteries of the first apostles, joined as they are in their brotherly fellowship, apart from one another.[3]

Here, although the king's role in donating the land and ordering the foundation of the monastery is noted, the narrative is dominated by Benedict Biscop, the founder of Wearmouth. He receives the Jarrow estate from the king, and sends monks there under the leadership of Ceolfrid. A year later he builds a new monastery, at the royal behest.

A shorter account, similar in most respects, but with slight difference in the detail, is presented in what is usually regarded as Bede's source, the anonymous *Life of Ceolfrid*:[4]

Eight years after they had begun to found the aforementioned monastery [Wearmouth], it pleased king Ecgfrith for the redemption of his soul to give another forty hides of land to the most reverend abbot Benedict, on which the church and monastery of the blessed Paul was to be built [i.e. Jarrow]; and it was not to be separated from the community of the first monastery, but joined to it in all respects in harmonious brotherly love. Ceolfrid very energetically carried out this task, which was committed to him; he received twenty-two brothers, ten of them tonsured and twelve still awaiting the grace of the tonsure, and came to the place.[5]

4

The *Life of Ceolfrid* goes on to further emphasise Ecgfrith's role in the development of Jarrow by stating that the king chose the site for the church's altar[6] – a detail which Bede omits. Among the other differences between this account and that of Bede is the absence of any distinction between the first year of a community at Jarrow and the subsequent foundation of a monastery, as mentioned in the *Historia Abbatum*. The initial number of monks also varies. In both narratives, however, Biscop is a dominant figure, whereas he makes no appearance on the Jarrow dedication stone.

Strictly speaking, of course, the descriptions in Bede and the anonymous *Vita Ceolfridi* concern the foundation of the monastery, while the dedication stone relates solely to the church. Thus, it is just possible to combine the information into a unified account: Biscop can be seen as the founder, and Ecgfrith as the builder. Rather harder to square with the inscription is the statement in the *Vita Ceolfridi* that Biscop himself ruled Jarrow for eight years before his death, in other words from the monastery's foundation.[7] Surely an abbot would have some say in the building of his monastic church. Biscop's lack of involvement is highlighted by the fact that he was not even in England at the time of the church's consecration – since he was currently on one of his visits to Rome, which lasted at least two years, from 684.[8] The differences between the narrative accounts and the dedication stone itself have caused some raised eyebrows, but little more, and the most recent solution has been to suggest that part of the inscription is missing.[9] I have to say that I find this proposition difficult to accept, and would rather reconsider the problem within the context of the early years of the monastery at Jarrow.

King Ecgfrith and *Nechtanesmere*

It is worth starting by considering the date of the dedication: 23rd April 685. The next major event in Northumbrian history took place less than a month later, on 21st May, according to Bede: the *Annals of Ulster* give a date of the 20th May.[10] It was the death of Ecgfrith at the Battle of *Nectanesmere*, near Aberlemno, to the north of the River Tay. The battle of *Nechtanesmere* itself was described in the *Life of Wilfrid* by Stephanus as 'a most woeful disaster in which Ecgfrith, King of the Northumbrians, had been slain and overthrown by the Picts, together with all the flower of his army.'[11] It is only a guess, but a very plausible one, that Ecgfrith was at the dedication of Jarrow. Not only is his name on the dedication stone, but according to the anonymous author of the *Vita Ceolfridi* (though not to Bede) the king chose the spot on which the altar should be placed. The distance from Jarrow to *Nechtanesmere* is substantial, but by no means an impossible journey for a month. Besides, we may also guess that Ecgfrith went by sea. He could easily have taken a ship from Jarrow Slake, the area that now lies just across the River Don, under the car park for the Nissan car plant. In Bede's day the river would have run along the southern edge of the Slake, which would thus have been directly accessible from the monastery. At a time when boats would normally have been pulled up onto dry, or tidal ground, and not moored at a quayside, this was one of the great natural harbours of the North of England (fig 1). Edwin Gifford, the master-mariner who built the half-scale replica of the Sutton Hoo ship, has described it as an 'ideal winter mud-berth'.[12] We will return to the harbour at Jarrow, but for the time-being I suggest that the dedication of Jarrow was Ecgfrith's last official engagement before his fatal trip north.

6

We know a surprising amount about the period surrounding the battle of *Nechtanesmere*, which may suggest that it was thought to be a time of some significance. Indeed the cluster of evidence, which crops up across a number of sources is surely an indication that the months on either side of the battle impacted greatly on the imagination of contemporaries. The crisis in many respects begins the year before, in 684, when Ecgfrith ordered an attack on Ireland, which may perhaps be associated with the presence of his half-brother Aldfrith 'among the islands of the Irish'.[13] Although the Irish are said to have resisted the invasion, the expedition was partially successful, in so far as a large number of Irish prisoners seem to have been brought back to Northumbria.[14] Nevertheless, the expedition was not well regarded even by some Anglo-Saxons. Bede records opposition from the holy man Ecgbert, then resident in Ireland. He also attributes the failure of the Pictish campaign to divine displeasure over the king's earlier actions. Criticism of the attack on the Picts came from closer to home, notably from bishop Cuthbert, but also from the king's friends.[15]

The king was surely aware of the dangers of a major campaign against his northern neighbours: in the *Lives of Cuthbert* we are told that Ecgfrith's wife Iurminburg went to stay in her sister's nunnery in Carlisle while waiting for news of the battle.[16] It is certainly worth asking why the queen had gone about as far from the east coast of Northumbria as possible: there must have been anxieties about her remaining in what one would normally have regarded as the centre of the kingdom, Bamburgh and the heartlands of Northumbria, which I will argue should be understood in this period to be the valley of the River Tyne.[17] Instead she had gone to her sister in the west. One wonders also whether Ecgfrith himself had kin in the Carlisle region – unfortunately we do not know for sure whether his mother was Rieinmellt of Rheged or Eanfled:[18] if the former, he might well

8

Fig 1. Jarrow Slake and the River Don.
Ordnance Survey, 1862

9

have had relatives in the neighbourhood: the latter, in any case, seems also to have had connections with Rheged.[19] The ninth-century *Historia Brittonum* apparently claims that Ecgfrith and Iurminburg had at least one son, Oslac,[20] so we may wonder whether the queen was also protecting their offspring. On the other hand, if the queen were indeed in Carlisle for her own safety, Cuthbert's advice, following his vision of the king's death is extremely curious. According to Bede, the saint told the queen, 'See that you mount your chariot early on Monday – for it is not lawful to travel by chariot on the Lord's Day – and go and enter the royal city quickly, lest perchance the king has been slain.'[21] If the royal city is, as usually assumed, Bamburgh, she would seem to be heading towards danger.[22]

We are on safer ground when we look at what happened after *Nechtanesmere*: Ecgfrith's half-brother, Aldfrith returned from his exile in Ireland. We are told that he 'ably restored the shattered state of the kingdom although within narrower bounds.'[23] He also seems to have instituted a new pro-Irish policy, for within a year the abbot of Iona, Adomnán, took sixty captives back to Ireland: presumably they had been taken during Ecgfrith's raid.[24] It is perhaps in this context that we need to set the rather surprising evidence supplied by the early twelfth-century writer Symeon of Durham, that Ecgfrith was buried on Iona.[25] This seems rather surprising in that Ecgfrith had no obvious links with the Scots of Dalriata, and the attack on Ireland is unlikely to have endeared him to the Columban community. If we accept Symeon's words, we might guess that Aldfrith negotiated the burial. One might envisage a complicated diplomatic arrangement, in which the release of Irish captives attested in the sources was made in return for the Iona community caring for the king's body.[26] Aldfrith and Adomnán would have been ideally placed to make such a deal.[27] And Aldfrith might have been only too pleased that he did not have to arrange for his half-brother to be buried in Northumbria. The return of a prince who had been in exile thus marked a major shift in policy. Although Ecgfrith's death had not led to a change to another ruling dynasty, there was clearly a substantial political reorientation.

The new foundation of Jarrow

It is worth pausing to consider what all this must have meant for the new foundation of Jarrow. The land on which the monastery was founded had been provided by Ecgfrith at a time when there was considerable opposition to his policies – though Bede is careful to separate his narrative of these from what he has to say of Benedict Biscop and of the king's involvement in the new monastery.[28] Jarrow's main church was dedicated less than a month before the king's death. Ecgfrith's name is on the dedication stone. Strictly speaking it is only there to provide a date, although we may ask whether readers of the inscription were not meant to understand more than that, especially given the king's role in choosing the site for the church's altar. Certainly, in the *Life of Ceolfrid* and Bede's *Historia Abbatum*, royal involvement in the foundation of the monastery is overshadowed by Biscop's contribution, but it is, nevertheless, acknowledged. Effectively Jarrow was a royal foundation.[29] The Battle of *Nechtanesmere*, according to Bede, shattered the kingdom, which had to be restored by Ecgfrith's exiled half-brother. One can well believe that the period after *Nechtanesmere* was one of more than a little worry for the monastery.

We might, however, conclude that the effect on Jarrow would have been slight: we are, after all, repeatedly told that the monastery was a sister-house of the already well-established Wearmouth. Indeed, according to Bede and to the author of the *Life of Ceolfrid*, the two monasteries were intended from the start to constitute an integrated double-house.[30] As a result we might assume that Jarrow was well placed to weather the storm. At this point, however, I think we should return to the dedication stone. It gives no hint that the house was intended to be a Siamese twin for Wearmouth, except possibly for the fact that it was dedicated to St Paul, while the older house was dedicated to St Peter. As we have already noted, there is no reference in the inscription to Benedict Biscop. This silence may seem less accidental when we remember that he had gone abroad at the time of the dedication of what we are usually told was his church.[31] This observation ought to make us stop and think, especially since at the time of the establishment of Wearmouth he explicitly waited in Northumbria until all was complete, before going to Rome.[32]

We may, however, think that mention of Ceolfrid in the inscription is enough to suggest that the foundation of Jarrow was indeed overseen by Biscop. Ceolfrid had, after all, been a monk at Biscop's Wearmouth. Yet we should also remember that he had made at least one attempt to leave – something that Bede passes over, but which is recounted by the anonymous author of the *Vita Ceolfridi*.[33] Perhaps when Ecgfrith suggested the creation of a new monastery on the Jarrow estate Ceolfrid was only too happy to move to new pastures. Biscop might not have been in a position to do more than acquiesce in a royal decision which Ceolfrid was willing to carry out. As we have seen, the inscription leaves out Biscop altogether, and implies that the only figures involved are Ceolfrid and the king. There is thus no hint that we are dealing with an offshoot of Wearmouth. Should we perhaps take the stone at face value, and see the later, perhaps hysterical, insistence that Jarrow was intended to be joined to Wearmouth from the start,[34] as an attempt to cover up the point that initially Jarrow was an independent foundation? Certainly the hectoring tone of both the author of the *Life of Ceolfrid* and Bede suggests that the two of them were intent on contradicting an opposing view which was well known, whether or not that opinion was correct. Should we conclude that Jarrow was only amalgamated with Wearmouth in the aftermath of Ecgfrith's death?

We can be reasonably sure that Jarrow was founded with monks from Wearmouth, and that its first abbot, Ceolfrid, was taken from there. On the other hand there are indications that not all the first monks at Jarrow were transferred from Biscop's monastery. In his description of the initial liturgical arrangements at Jarrow the anonymous author of the *Vita Ceolfridi* remarks that 'He [Ceolfrid] adopted all the same practices of singing and reading which they had kept in the first monastery, to be kept there also, even though by no means all those who came there with him were acquainted with singing the psalms, and even less familiar with reading in the church and saying the antiphons and responses.'[35] One might argue that were Wearmouth and Jarrow to have been a single foundation Ceolfrid would not have had the option of choosing the type of liturgy to be followed. Equally important, any monk from Wearmouth would have known the liturgical arrangements, which, as we have seen, some did not. In other words not all the new monks can have come from Wearmouth. This may be a factor underlying the conflict between the numbers of original monks provided: 17 according to Bede[36] and 22 according to the anonymous.[37] Again, if the two monasteries had indeed been one, the statement in the *Vita Ceolfridi* that on the death of abbot Eosterwine of Wearmouth 'the brothers appointed as abbot Sicgfrid', with the simple rider that 'abbot Ceolfrid also advised them on this' is slightly puzzling.[38] One would have expected Ceolfrid to have played a more important role in the appointment of his fellow abbot. Although in time the two houses would be joined under a single abbot, that was not the case until some years after Eosterwine died.

There is, perhaps, one further indication that Jarrow was essentially on its own at the time of Ecgfrith's death. The anonymous author of the *Life of Ceolfrid* records that at the time of the death of abbot Eosterwine at Wearmouth the plague which killed him also struck Jarrow, where only Ceolfrid and a single boy were fit enough to perform the liturgy.[39] This story has become particularly famous because, I now think rightly, Bede has been identified as the young boy.[40] Concentration on the identification of Ceolfrid's young helper, however, has, I believe, led us to ignore more important aspects of the story. Why, if Wearmouth and Jarrow were a single house, was Ceolfrid left with only one small helper in the liturgy? Why did he not just ask for brothers from down the road? But consider the date. John of Worcester dated the death of Eosterwine to 685.[41] Plummer reckoned that to be a year too early.[42] Either way, the plague struck Jarrow at the time of *Nechtanesmere* or just afterwards – at a moment, that is, immediately or not long after the death of its royal benefactor. I would suggest that, regardless of whether or not Bede was the young boy, Ceolfrid was struggling, not just because of the plague, but also because Jarrow was suffering from its association with Ecgfrith immediately after the king's death. This was, after all, a time when Aldfrith, the half-brother whom Ecgfrith had so desperately opposed, was establishing himself as king.

Since Wearmouth and Jarrow were not quite as close at the time of the foundation of the younger house as Bede would have us think, we should ask when they did draw closer together. We know that Benedict Biscop did a deal with Aldfrith as soon as he returned from his trip to Rome and found a new government in place. When he returned he used two silk stoles (*pallia*) of considerable value that he had brought with him to acquire land to the south of the Wear from the new king and his thegns.[43] Bede seems to imply some connection between

Biscop's discovery of Ecgfrith's death and the acquisition of the land, though the link may only be chronological. Thereafter first Biscop and then Ceolfrid negotiated with Aldfrith over the acquisition of land on the River *Fresca*.[44] Were these the only deals Biscop did? Aldfrith would not have been sorry to see his half-brother's foundation swallowed by a neighbouring house.

It is, however, possible to argue that it was not until the time of Biscop's death that the two houses were fully amalgamated. According to the anonymous *Vita Ceolfridi*, when Biscop was dying, he discussed the question of the succession 'with the brothers [of Wearmouth], summoned Ceolfrid and appointed him abbot of both monasteries, decreeing that it should be a single foundation in every way, even though it was located in two places, always guided by a single abbot, kept safe by the protection of the same privilege.'[45] The implication of this would seem to be that the two houses had previously not been 'a single foundation in every way'. In terms of canon law it is unlikely that they could have been so regarded. Despite Biscop's appeal to a papal privilege, the grant in question is likely only to have been relevant to Wearmouth, having been made by pope Agatho c. 679-80 before the foundation of Jarrow. A subsequent privilege secured from pope Sergius by Ceolfrid c. 701 may have been concerned solely with the younger monastery.[46] In any case, the author of the *Vita Ceolfridi* waits until Biscop's death until he states that 'Ceolfrid undertook the care of both monasteries, or rather of the one monastery in two locations'.[47] Bede makes the same point when, in narrating Biscop's last days, he says that Benedict

thought it would be very salutary in every way for maintaining the peace, unity and harmony of the two places if they had one father-abbot and ruler in perpetuity, often calling to mind the example of the kingdom of Israel, which always remained undamaged and unconquerable by foreign nations so long as it

15

was ruled by a single leader from that same people; but after it was split apart in a hateful internal struggle because its sins overtook it, it perished little by little, and struck down from its position of security it became extinct.[48]

In other words full union did not take place until 688, and, as the final analogy with Israel suggests, it continued to be under threat.

This threat, I would suggest, was still a living issue at the time of the composition of the *Life of Ceolfrid* and Bede's *History of the Abbots*. That danger was ongoing is implied by the fact that just as Bede puts into Biscop's mouth a plea for unity, so too the anonymous author puts a similar plea into Ceolfrid's.[49] These statements were surely aimed at the readers of the hagiography, and were not simply historical records. What the divisions were is harder to establish. That family issues and inheritance rights were involved seems likely: according to Bede, Biscop was concerned to ensure that members of his family were not appointed to positions within his monasteries simply on the strength of their relationship with him. Indeed, he explicitly notes a threat from an earthly brother, *frater meus carnalis*.[50] And he goes on to state that 'those who raise sons according to the flesh in a fleshly manner have to look for fleshly heirs for their fleshly inheritance.' Bede's ugly repetition of the word *carnali/carnales*, 'fleshly', is clearly deliberate. Nevertheless, Biscop himself did promote relatives: Eosterwine was a cousin, while Ceolfrid was also related.[52] Family politics and demands may have lain behind some of the difficulties faced at Wearmouth and Jarrow, although in themselves they cannot account entirely for the potential problems for the two communities. Royal politics may have been another factor: both monasteries were founded on land given by Ecgfrith, and his successors may well have eyed the properties.[53] What seems clear is that the monasteries continued to act as separate entities, even under Ceolfrid.

16

One further indication of their separation is the fact that lands seem to have been acquired for one or other house, and not for both jointly, even in the period of Ceolfrid's sole abbacy. Thus, we are told by Bede that Ceolfrid acquired land on the river *Fresca* from Aldfrid for the monastery of St Paul.[54] Similarly Witmer brought with him the estate of *Daldun* for St Peter[55] – an estate that was still part of the Bishop Wearmouth lands in the tenth century.[56]

The two monasteries seem also to have been treated rather differently on the occasion of Ceolfrid's departure for Rome in 716. The abbot made no attempt to summon a joint gathering of the leading monks of both houses, but initially addressed the monks of St Peter's alone.[57] He told them to preserve unity with the monks of St Paul's.[58] The two houses could, however, act together, and did so in electing Hwætbert as abbot.[59] Yet even so Hwætbert, once elected, described himself to the pope as abbot of St Peter's.[60] Of course, this might just have been a shorthand. Yet one is left with the impression that whatever the unity was, it had not quite created a single community of Sts Peter and Paul.

A similar impression may be derived from later documentation: Alcuin wrote four letters to Wearmouth-Jarrow. One is addressed to abbot Friduin:[61] another is addressed to the monks of both communities:[62] but, in addition, there is one letter to Jarrow,[63] and one to St Peter's, that is to Wearmouth.[64] Whatever the union of the two houses added up to, it still allowed the separate units to retain some individual identity. That this individuality could theoretically stretch to division, at least as late the 720s is implied by the recurrent pleas for unity given to both Biscop and Ceolfrid in the *Vita Ceolfridi* and Bede's *Historia Abbatum*.

The notion that Jarrow was not originally intended to be joined to Wearmouth is hypothesis, although much surrounding the hypothesis is clear enough, at least by the standards of the seventh century. The end of Ecgfrith's reign was a crisis period that must have impinged on Jarrow. We may be able to say a little more about the monastery's early years if we turn to some rather later evidence, and in particular if we reconsider some awkward questions.

Jarrow and the mouth of the Tyne

In a characteristically learned footnote Charles Plummer stated that 'S[ymeon]. [of] D[urham]. calls Jarrow 'portus Ecgfridi regis,' i. 51; and the [Anglo-Saxon] Chron[icle]. calls the monastery 'Ecgferthes mynster.' 794 D.E.'[65] For various reasons Plummer's statement has been undermined in recent years. It is necessary to consider whether it has actually been proved to be false.[66]

Symeon of Durham unquestionably referred to Viking attacks on a monastery at the mouth of the Don and on the harbour of Ecgfrith, which he glossed as Jarrow: he states that the heathen 'were ravaging the port of King Ecgfrith (that is Jarrow) and pillaging also the monastery at the mouth of the river Don.'[67] The same information is to be founded in the *Historia Regum*, once, and possibly correctly, attributed to Symeon,[68] where the gloss identifying the harbour as Jarrow is omitted, but a date of 794 is supplied.[69] A similar account is to be found in Roger of Howden, who, like Symeon, had access to northern materials.[70] In addition, a variant in which there is no mention of a harbour, but where the monastery is ascribed to Ecgfrith appears in two manuscripts of the *Anglo-Saxon Chronicle* and in several Latin histories, including that of Henry of Huntingdon.[71]

It has rightly been noted that Symeon is our only source identifying the *Portus Ecgfridi* as Jarrow, and the lack of corroboration has been held to cast doubt on the identification.

So too, the fact that the river which runs past Jarrow is only known to have been called the Don since the sixteenth century has raised suspicions that it was not so called in Bede's day.[72] In recent years there have also been two important discussions of the identity of the monastery at the mouth of the Don, which have placed it at one site or another in the south side of the Humber basin, on the Yorkshire Don.[73] Nevertheless, there are problems with placing Ecgfrith's harbour and monastery to the south of the Humber. In 679 Ecgfrith's ambitions in Southumbria were checked at a battle on the River Trent. This was to be a significant moment in the limitation of the Northumbrian kingdom to the region north of the Humber.[74] A royal foundation south of the Humber in Ecgfrith's reign is not obviously very likely – certainly not in the later part of it. Nor is a major harbour in Southumbria likely to have been remembered by the name of a Northumbrian king. The possibility that we should be looking at another Ecgfrith has been put forward, and the name indeed was borne by the son of the Mercian king Offa.[75] Unfortunately, Offa's son cannot have been old enough to have given his name to the monastery at the mouth of the Don, if one assumes that there was only one monastery known as *Donemutha*, since it is referred to in a papal letter of 757-8.[76] Further, the papal letter is addressed to Eadbert of Northumbria, and can only be concerned with territory in the northern kingdom at that time. We have, I think, to conclude that Symeon's harbour of Ecgfrith and the monastery on the Don were to be found north of the Humber. We need to reconsider Symeon's identification of the site as Jarrow.

The arguments against the identification are first, that had Jarrow been sacked by the Vikings in 794, Alcuin would surely have said as much, because of his reverence for Bede.[77] This is probably true, though it would be absurd to think that all

Alcuin's letters have survived, and thus an argument based entirely on silence is scarcely secure. Moreover, one might note that, while Alcuin refers to Bede's upbringing at Jarrow in his poem on the bishops, kings and saints of York,[78] in his letters he explicitly links him with Wearmouth.[79] For him the association of Bede and Jarrow may not have been as strong as we take it to be.

Second, it has been argued that it is curious that the sack of such an important monastery is not mentioned in other sources. Again this is a plausible argument, although one should note that the name Jarrow, *Gyrwe* or *In Gyruum*, is very rarely used anyway. Bede tends to talk of the monastery of St Paul, making no use of a word for Jarrow in his hagiography, and only using one twice in the *Ecclesiastical History*.[80] Alcuin uses a Latin version of the name twice in his letters and once in his York poem.[81] It is, therefore, possible that attacks on Jarrow are referred to, but under another name. Hence the longstanding acceptance of the identification of the monastery of *Donemutha* with Jarrow.

It is necessary to return to the papal letter of 757/8. There we discover that an abbess had given the three monasteries of *Staningagrave* (Stonegrave), *Cuchawalda* (Coxwold) and *Donemutha* to an abbot called Forthred,[82] but that king Eadbert had taken them and redistributed them to Æthelwold Moll, who was the brother of either the abbess[83] or of Forthred. It has been argued that the *Donemutha* in this letter cannot have been Jarrow because the latter was not a double house under an abbess. The letter, however, says nothing about the constitution of the monastery, or how it came into the hands of the abbess. As we have seen, the official unity of Wearmouth[84] and Jarrow was not above question. Moreover, the abbess could conceivably have gained Jarrow through inheritance rights. We have already noted that Benedict Biscop was exceedingly worried as to whether members of his family would lay claim to Wearmouth.

Jarrow, founded on royal land, would have been no more safe. In the papal letter we could be seeing evidence to show that Biscop's fears were well founded. We can, after all, identify Wearmouth-Jarrow's abbots for the years 746-7 when Boniface wrote to abbot Hwætbert,[85] and 763-4 when Lull wrote to abbot Cuthbert,[86] but not for the intervening years. The pope's intervention over *Donemutha* occurred in 757/8, inconveniently in a period when we know nothing of Jarrow or its abbot. One might also argue that the intervention of the king, Eadbert, and the transfer of the monastery to his brother, would be perfectly in keeping with the fact that Jarrow was founded on what had been royal land. One might guess that Stonegrave and Coxwold were also royal foundations:[87] that would explain the grouping of all three in the papal letter. The arguments against the identification of *Donemutha* and Jarrow, in other words, are not insuperable. It is possible to recast our understanding of Jarrow as a royal house, which continued to be subject to inheritance disputes, just as Biscop had feared.

In short, the argument that *Donemutha* was not Jarrow is, I think, less strong than has been assumed in recent years. On the other hand, it may be that we should envisage another, smaller house, situated closer to the Don mouth, which in Bede's day lay some way to the east of Jarrow. We need to remember quite how different the lower Tyne looked, before the dumping of vast amounts of ballast along its banks, and before the creation of docks in the nineteenth century – let alone the transformation of the remains of Jarrow Slake into a car park in the late twentieth. Indeed early maps show that before the creation of Tyne Dock, the Don entered the Tyne effectively at High Shields. It is to the east rather than to the west of Jarrow Slake that we should place *Donemutha* (fig 2).

That Jarrow did not control all the land between the monastery and the coast is suggested by the famous story in Bede's *Life of*

Cuthbert in which monks crossing the Tyne were nearly washed out to sea. Bede's description goes as follows: 'Now there is a monastery not far from the mouth of the Tyne, on the south side, filled with a noble company, in those days of men but now, changed like all else by time, of virgins who serve Christ.'[88] This fits exactly with our requirements:[89] a house, initially of monks, between Jarrow and the sea. It was transferred to nuns even in Bede's day, and certainly before the letter of Pope Paul to Eadbert. Indeed, Bede has a little more to tell us about its history as a nunnery, for he talks of Verca who was abbess of a house 'situated not far from the mouth of the river Tyne', who was visited by Cuthbert, and who indeed gave him the cloth in which he was later to be buried.[90] Cuthbert who, thus, could be found hanging around the Lower Tyne as a child, kept in contact with the area. That the nunnery was given by one of the successors of abbess Verca to abbot Forthred, before the king transferred it from him to Æthelwold Moll, is thus no problem. Nor are we left to explain away the silence of Alcuin or of other sources over a Viking raid on Bede's monastery. This nunnery situated between Jarrow and the sea should, I would suggest, be identified as *Donemutha*. Probably it should be sought close to the old mouth of the Don, at the edge of the vicus of the Roman fort of *Arbeia* (assuming that name to have been correctly apportioned to the excavations in South Shields).

One might ask whether the monastery of *Donemutha* lay in the Roman fort itself. The most recent excavations neither help nor hinder such a hypothesis.[91] On the other hand re-examination of old finds has turned up material compatible with the identification of Arbeia as a high-status site in the Anglo-Saxon period.[92] There is, moreover, a tantalising reference in Leland's *Collectanea* to a site which has been identified as *Arbeia*: 'in the region of Tynemouth there was a city called *Urfa*, which was destroyed by the Danes: there king Oswine was born.'[93]

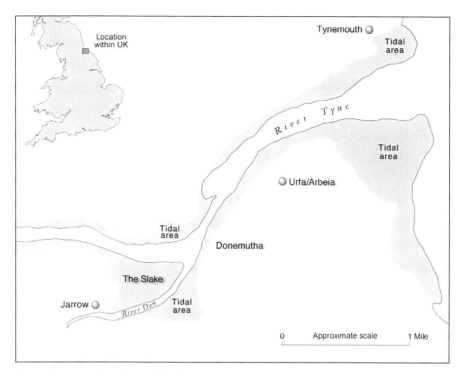

Fig 2. Jarrow and the Mouth of the River Tyne (source: I.N. Wood, 'Monasteries and the geography of power in the Age of Bede', Northern History 45, 2008)

Linguistically *Urfa* is a perfectly plausible development of *Arbeia*.[94] The implication would seem to be that the site was a royal residence at the time of Oswine's birth in the early seventh century.[95] On the face of it this is possible, although it may initially seem surprising that Oswine, a Deiran, related to Edwin, should have been born so far north.[96] In considering the northern associations of the Deirans, however, it should be noted that Hild began her monastic career north of the Wear, before moving to Hartlepool and, only ultimately, to Whitby.[97]

In any case there are other indications that Oswine should be linked with the region, and they indeed suggest a further royal monastery across the river at Tynemouth. Unfortunately they come from the High Middle Ages or later. A *Passio*, which was written by a monk of St Albans in the early twelfth century claimed that Oswine was buried at Tynemouth.[98] The author of this *Passio* had access to local tradition, having spent part of his monastic career in the northern monastery.[99] The information on Oswine's burial is repeated by two other St Albans monks, Roger of Wendover and Matthew Paris, who date the burial to the year 651.[100] Both seem to have had access to a *Passio* of the king other than that already mentioned. The interest of St Albans is easily explained, since Tynemouth was one of its dependent cells.[101] Moreover, the tradition of history-writing at St Albans was second to none. On the other hand, this does not guarantee that the information on Oswine was genuine. It is possible that monks of St Albans deliberately created evidence for a martyr cult in one of their cells.[102]

In the sixteenth century Leland mentioned a *Vita* of Oswine as well as a chronicle by an anonymous monk of St Albans.[103] These references could be to the *Vita Oswini* already mentioned, and to the chronicle of either Roger of Wendover or Matthew Paris. Yet Leland also had additional information on the foundation of the monastery, which the nineteenth-century local historian W.S. Gibson claimed had come from another *Vita* of Oswine. He identified the source as being Corpus Christi College, Oxford, MS 134, a remarkable compilation of material relating to the cult of the Anglo-Saxon king.[104] According to Leland, Tynemouth was founded by Edwin, and it was rebuilt in stone by Oswald.[105] Neither statement sounds plausible, since this would make the monastery the earliest monastic foundation in the North, and would suggest the building of a stone monastery earlier than Ripon.[106] In addition Leland notes the burial of another 'Deiran' king, 'Edred', at Tynemouth.[107] Exactly who he was is unclear, though there are three Eadreds to choose from in the list of kings and war-leaders, *reges* and *duces*, in the *Liber Vitae* of Durham.[108] Some of the detail purveyed by Leland and the St Albans authors is certainly suspect. All that we can say is that there was a tradition that Tynemouth was associated with royalty. Nevertheless, we can be much more confident over the evidence of the *Anglo-Saxon Chronicle* that indicates a third royal burial at Tynemouth, that of Osred, who was buried there in 792.[109] Since the monastery would seem to have been used for royal burials, one might wonder if there was any deliberate symbolism in its being sited on the north side of the river, directly across from a palace.[110]

Kings would have wanted to control the entrance to the Tyne, and with the north bank of the river occupied by the monastery of Tynemouth, the use of *Arbeia* as a secular strong point would seem an absolute requirement. Further, since Jarrow Slake provided an ideal harbour for early medieval ships, it would be surprising if there were no royal residence in the immediate vicinity: Arbeia would have been an obvious location. In the Roman period its maritime importance was clear from the fact that it housed a squadron of boatmen, the *numerus barcariorum Tigrisiensium*.[111] It would not have been an inappropriate birth-place for a prince like Oswine. Although a king may have decided to found a monastery within the fort, it is so obviously a strategic site, that we are probably safer locating *Donemutha* between *Arbeia* and the Don, rather than within the Roman fort.[112]

There is more to be gained from consideration of the sources that refer to the monastery on the Don. It is worth noting the difference between the accounts of Symeon of Durham and Roger of Howden – both of them writers with access to good northern tradition[113] – on the one hand and the *Anglo-Saxon Chronicle* and other sources on the other. The former two sources make a distinction between Ecgfrith's harbour and the monastery on the Don, while the latter talk only of the

25

monastery of *Donemutha* or, in the cases of the E manuscript of the Chronicle and of Henry of Huntingdon, of Ecgfrith's monastery at *Donemutha*.[114] It seems to me that this second group of texts has collapsed two sites which Symeon and Roger kept apart: the harbour and the monastery. If we place *Donemutha* directly to the east of the River Don, we can easily accept that Symeon had reason to identify Ecgfrith's harbour with Jarrow Slake. Since the E manuscript of the Anglo-Saxon Chronicle describes the monastery at *Donemutha* as *Ecgferthes mynster* we must assume that the king's involvement in the house was considerable: after all his name is not associated with his foundation at Jarrow, even though it is broadcast on the dedication inscription. It would thus appear that the Slake was overlooked from both the east and the west by monasteries associated with Ecgfrith.[115] No wonder it was called *Portus Ecgfridi*.[116]

This set of identifications tells us a good deal about the south bank of the Tyne, between Jarrow and the sea. Ecgfrith founded St Paul's monastery overlooking his harbour, which lay on Jarrow Slake. The monastery itself was royal, in that it was founded on land that had belonged to the king, and also in that Ecgfrith himself had commissioned the building of the church of St Paul. We can imagine that the monks said prayers for his sailors. In Bede's day the Don flowed to the far side of the Slake: beyond that lay another monastery, which was transformed into a community of nuns. It was this community which became known as *Donemutha*, and it was this together with the harbour, that the Vikings sacked. Further, by the time of the Viking raid *Donemutha* would appear to have been known as *Ecgferth's mynster*,[117] indicating that the king was either responsible for its initial foundation, or more probably, since the house already existed when Cuthbert was still a boy, its transformation into a female house. Perhaps the two

26

monasteries were connected by a causeway across the Slake, like the pairs of monasteries in the Witham valley.[118] If we can accept Leland's evidence, beyond *Donemutha*, in *Arbeia*, there was a royal centre, *Urfa*, which would be destroyed by the Vikings may be at the same time as the nunnery.[119]

For there to have been two monasteries of importance in such proximity, one each on either side of Jarrow Slake is remarkable.[120] So too is the fact that Bede makes only one passing reference to the nunnery which lay within sight of his own monastery. Yet both houses seem to have been dependent on the same royal benefactor. It may be worth airing some other possibilities that could have impacted on the relation of the two houses. *Donemutha* must have been the earlier of the two foundations, since the story about the monks crossing the Tyne relates to Cuthbert's childhood.[121] Bede's comment on the transfer of the house from men to women may contain a note of regret: in his words the monastery had been 'filled with a noble company, in those days of men, but now, changed like all else by time'.[122] Such transfers are not unusual,[123] but one might ask in each case what the particular significance of the transfer was. Had the monks been transferred to Jarrow, either at the time of the foundation of Ceolfrid's monastery, or shortly thereafter? Given the fact that the community was already in existence when Cuthbert was a child, probably before the accession of Ecgfrith, but that it was later known as Ecgferthes mynster, the transformation of *Donemutha* would seem to have taken place during the king's lifetime. If monks from there were transferred to Jarrow at the moment that the latter house was founded, they would have been among those who could not sing according to the practices established at Wearmouth.[124]

A further possibility is that Ecgfrith's queen Iurminburg had some interest in *Donemutha*. Bede is remarkably silent about her, never naming the queen, and only twice referring to her.[125] Stephanus, by contrast, talks of her on a number of occasions, and presents her as a vicious queen who came to see the error of her ways and to become a model abbess.[126] Although we do know from Bede that she took the veil at Carlisle, where she was blessed by Cuthbert, we do not know that she stayed there. We can reasonably assume that her consecration took place in her sister's abbey, but we do not know that it was there that she would become abbess. We might guess that geographically the setting in which she took the veil was convenient from Aldfrith's point of view, since it removed his sister-in-law from the centre of the kingdom. But his concerns may have changed over time. At the very least it would have been appropriate for her to have had an association with *Donemutha*, or rather with *Ecgferthes mynster*. What more appropriate nunnery for Iurminburg would there be, than a house that her husband had refounded as a community for women?

Conclusions

Like much that I have covered, this is hypothesis. On the other hand the issues we have dealt with seem to me to put Jarrow in a rather different light from that in which it is usually seen. Briefly to recap: the foundation of Jarrow, and more especially the dedication of St Paul's, took place during a period of political crisis. This must have impinged on the new foundation, not least because the king, Ecgfrith, who was at the centre of the crisis, was also the man who provided the land for the new monastery, which – let us put it at its mildest – was rather less associated with Benedict Biscop than the next generation claimed. Biscop, moreover, was very obviously absent from the dedication of St Paul's, whereas it is a reasonable guess that Ecgfrith himself was not. Further, we may guess that while the king was attending the dedication of St Paul's, his fleet was assembling on the nearby mud flats, which were to be known as the *Portus Ecgfridi*. On the far side of the harbour lay the community of *Donemutha*, perhaps recently transformed from a house of monks to a convent. We may also guess that the king exploited the occasion of the dedication: the new church itself would have been an indication of the piety of the warrior king,[127] and prayers would surely have been said for him and his fleet. Unfortunately Ecgfrith's immediate departure for Pictland was to lead to his own death and to disaster for the kingdom.

Had Ecgfrith himself ever stopped to think that St Paul's, overlooking his harbour, might have made a suitable mausoleum? The lower Tyne was certainly a region of royal burials: we have noted three possibilities at Tynemouth. The *Vita Ceolfridi* links the foundation of Jarrow explicitly with Ecgfrith's personal salvation.[128] We might even ask if his body could have been brought back from *Nechtanesmere* to Jarrow or to Ecgfrith's minster. Symeon of Durham, whose sources for Anglo-Saxon Northumbria were often good, states that the king was buried on Iona,[129] and, as we have seen, it might be possible to envisage a complicated diplomatic arrangement, in which the release of Irish captives attested in the sources was made in return for the Iona community caring for the king's body.[130] On the other hand, the dismemberment of the bodies of kings killed in battle was not uncommon,[131] and fragments could be distributed in different places. Were we to suppose that Ecgfrith's corpse, or part of it, was returned to Jarrow or *Donemutha*, we would have a particular reason for the association of the king's name with the harbour on Jarrow Slake.[132] A great church looking across a gathering place for the royal fleet would have been an appropriate resting place for a king with his aspirations. We may guess that sea-power was something of which he was very aware: his attack on Ireland in

684 must have required the services of a considerable number of ships.[133] On the other hand, if all Ecgfrith's remains had been taken to Iona, St Paul's or indeed *Donemutha* might have been regarded as the king's cenotaph.

A reasonable objection to this last argument might be the silence of Bede over the matter. However, it is worth remembering that *Nechtanesmere* had led to the elevation of Ecgfrith's exiled half-brother, Aldfrith, to the throne of Northumbria. It must also have led to some adjustments within Jarrow itself. I have suggested already that the four years between *Nechtanesmere* and Biscop's death were a period when closer ties with Wearmouth may have been instituted. During that time Jarrow would have had to rethink its attitude towards its chief benefactor, Ecgfrith, who gets a somewhat ambivalent press in Bede – certainly not the write-up that a founder might have expected from a historian of his foundation, though unlike his queen he at least gets a mention. He was now the king who, in his attack on Ireland, had 'wretchedly devastated a harmless race that had always been most friendly to the English.' He 'rashly took an army to ravage the kingdom of the Picts, against the urgent advice of his friends and particularly of Cuthbert, of blessed memory, who had recently been made bishop.'[134] We are not told here that it was Ecgfrith himself who had appointed Cuthbert – that information is withheld until a later chapter.[135] But we are told that 'those who were justly cursed for their wickedness quickly suffered the penalty of their guilt at the avenging hand of God.' One can see why it might be useful to downplay the king's role in the foundation of Jarrow. If Ecgfrith or any part of him had been buried at his foundation, it would be possible to explain the silence of Bede and the anonymous author of the *Vita Ceolfridi* in the light of the hostility to Ecgfrith in his last years. It is possible that Jarrow experienced tensions similar to some of those which arose when Oswald's body was taken to Bardney – though in that instance the monastery lay outside the dead man's kingdom.[136]

Even if the association of Iurminburg and *Donemutha* does not stand up to scrutiny, it is just worth pausing to emphasise the extent to which the Lower Tyne was a royal centre. The Tyne as a whole was a major cultural and political zone: away from the river mouth there were the foundations of Hexham and Corbridge, and even of Bywell, which may be the eighth-century foundation described in Æthelwulf's *De Abbatibus*.[137] On the lower Tyne, however, there were monasteries at Jarrow, founded on royal land, and Tynemouth, which was at least royal in the sense that Oswine, Eadbert and Osred seem to have been buried there.[138] Tynemouth also seems to have had an association with another royal monastery, Whitby, whose nuns fled there in the late ninth century.[139] In addition there was the nunnery at *Donemutha*, apparently founded or refounded by Ecgfrith, which later attracted the attention of Eadbert and Æthelwold Moll. And there was the royal harbour of Jarrow Slake, whose transfer to the Nissan car company begins in this reconstruction to look like an act not just of ecological, but also of historical vandalism. If *Arbeia* was not the site of *Donemutha*, but was rather a residence of kings, the royal aspects of the region are even clearer. This is a cluster of royal sites which almost stands comparison with those in the Merovingian heartlands of the Île de France, and is indeed much more compact. Traditionally, depending on the precise period in question, historians have seen either Bamburgh, with its religious counterpart of Lindisfarne, or York as the centre of the Northumbrian kingdom. Yet Bede associated no king after Oswiu with Bamburgh,[140] although he may have referred to the place when using the phrase 'the royal city', *regiam civitatem*, in the context of Ecgfrith's death.[141] There is one reference to a slightly later period in the *Vita Wilfridi*, where Stephanus tells us that

Aldfrith's son Osred was beseiged there.[142] Taken together, however, these references do not suggest that Bamburgh and Lindisfarne were any more important than was the Lower Tyne by the end of the seventh century.[143]

Having situated Jarrow in a world of politics and of military planning, I should like briefly to stress that this should condition our reading of Bede. Recent scholarship is absolutely right to emphasise Bede's pastoral and theological concerns, and to see them as being central to his historical writing as to his Biblical commentaries. At the same time I would insist that we should stress that he was writing in a centre which had very close connections with kings. This, indeed, is apparent in the *Historia Ecclesiastica*, and in other of Bede's works. We know that Bede wrote in the hope that he would catch the ear of the king: the preface to the *Historia Ecclesiastica* shows that he did just that. We should also remember that his writing must therefore respond to politics. I have touched very briefly on this issue in discussing some of Bede's comments on Ecgfrith, who is presented as no more than equal to Benedict Biscop in the account of the foundation of Jarrow in the *Historia Abbatum*. A major factor here may well have been Ecgfrith's posthumous reputation, as a king who led unwarranted campaigns against the Irish and Picts, which caused disaster for his own people. It would have suited Jarrow to play down its royal origins, especially during the reign of Ecgfrith's half-brother, and rival, Aldfrith.

In recent years historians have seen in Bede a more politically aware commentator than used to be the case.[144] I would like to add to this awareness the matter of Jarrow's relation to the *Portus Ecgfridi*. Wearmouth-Jarrow did not just have close connections to the royal court, the northern of the two houses was also adjacent to what seems to have been thought of as a royal harbour – and we can guess that kings did not give up using it after Ecgfrith's death. What we mean by a royal harbour is an open question. That it was a place for gathering a fleet when the king needed it is one assumption I have made but this would have been a relatively rare occurrence. More usually it would have been a port with all the implications that that has for trade. When the Vikings attacked the *Portus Ecgfridi* it is unlikely that they did so to in order to destroy a royal fleet: rather they must have had their eye on the plunder to be taken from a functioning market. The proximity of such a site would have meant that Jarrow was not unlike some other monastic sites, such as Whitby, that are now known to have been situated close to trading places. This would surely have impinged on Bede's consciousness. Indeed, one might wonder whether Bede's interest in the tides was encouraged by the proximity of the harbour.[145] Their rise and fall would have attracted him in any case – since anyone spending their life on the banks of the lower Tyne, Wear or Don would have noticed them. The comings and goings on Jarrow Slake, however, would have reinforced his awareness.

Jarrow, I think, impinges more on Bede than we often realise. Of course as a scholar he transcended the place in which he worked, even the library which Biscop and Ceolfrid had established. Yet Jarrow had been a royal estate. Political and family interests in the site did not go away once it had been alienated to the Church. They must serve as a background to Bede's historical and hagiographical writing. Jarrow deserves attention, not just as Bede's home for much of his working life, but also as an important centre in the Northumbrian kingdom.

Notes

1   See I.N. Wood, *The Most Holy Abbot Ceolfrid*, Jarrow Lecture, 1995 (Newcastle-upon-Tyne, 1996), p. 1. This article is in many ways a return to aspects of the earlier lecture, prompted by preparation of a commentary for Chris Grocock's new edition of Bede's *Historia Abbatum* and the anonymous *Vita Ceolfridi*. A shorter version of it has already appeared as "Bede's Jarrow', in C.A. Lees and G.R. Overring, *A Place to Believe In* (University Park, Pennsylvania, 2006), pp. 67-84. I should like to thank Colm O'Brien and Laura Sole particularly for advice on maps of the Lower Tyne.

2   The calculations of C. Plummer, *Baedae Opera Historica* (Oxford, 1896), II, p. 361 and P. Hunter-Blair, *The World of Bede*, revised ed. (Cambridge, 1990), p. 176, differ slightly, but come to the same conclusion for the date of dedication.

3   Bede, *Historia Abbatum*, 7, ed. Plummer, *Baedae Opera Historica*. The translations of this text and the anonymous *Vita Ceolfridi* are based on those being prepared by Grocock for the new edition and translation of the texts in question. The account is discussed by Hunter-Blair, *The Age of Bede*, pp. 175-83.

4   If the boy in *Vita Ceolfridi*, 14, ed. Plummer, *Baedae Opera Historica*, is to be identified with Bede, it would seem from the text that he had already written about Ceolfrid.

5   *Vita Ceolfridi*, 11.

6   *Vita Ceolfridi*, 12.

7   *Vita Ceolfridi*, 18.

8   Bede, *Historia Abbatum*, 9: *Vita Ceolfridi*, 12, 15: see Plummer's note, *Baedae Opera Historica*, p. 372. The *Vita Ceolfridi* obscures the fact that Biscop was not in England by placing the description of the building and consecration of Jarrow before his departure.

9   J. Higgitt, 'The dedication inscription at Jarrow and its context', *Antiquaries Journal* 59 (1979), pp. 343-74, esp. 344, 352.

10   Bede, *Historia Ecclesiastica*, IV 26: *Annals of Ulster*, s.a. 686 (=685), ed. S. Mac Airt and G. Mac Niocaill (Dublin, 1983).

11   Stephanus, *Vita Wilfridi*, 44, ed. B. Colgrave, *The Life of Bishop Wilfrid by Eddius Stephanus* (Cambridge, 1927).

12   Personal communication from Chris Grocock.

13   Bede, *Historia Ecclesiastica*, IV 26: id., Vita Cuthberti, 24, ed. B. Colgrave, *Two Lives of Saint Cuthbert* (Cambridge, 1940): T.M. Charles-Edwards, *Early Christian Ireland* (Cambridge, 2000), pp. 432-3.

14   *Annals of Ulster*, 687 (=686): the captives returned by Adomnán are plausibly those taken by Ecgfrith's army.

15   Bede, *Historia Ecclesiastica*, IV 26.

16   Anon., *Vita Cuthberti*, IV 8, ed. Colgrave, *Two Lives of Saint Cuthbert*: Bede, *Vita Cuthberti*, 27.

17   See also I.N. Wood, 'Monasteries and the geography of power in the Age of Bede', *Northern History* 45 (2008), pp. 1-15, where I suggest that the centre of power of the *Bernicii* was on the lower Tyne and the Deiri in the Vale of Pickering.

18   C. Phythian-Adams, *Land of the Cumbrians: a study in British provincial origins A.D. 400-1120* (Aldershot, 1996), p. 60, suggests that Alhfrith was Rieinmellt's only son.

19   Phythian-Adams, *Land of the Cumbrians*, p. 60, identifies Ecgfrith as Eanfled's son: pp. 98-9 stresses the involvement of Rhun, son of Urien, in her baptism: for the evidence, *Historia Brittonum* 63, in Nennius, *British History and the Welsh Annals*, ed. J. Morris (London, 1980).

20   *Historia Brittonum* 61. Morris, p. 37, emends the text to make Aelfwin the father of Oslac, but see Phythian-Adams, *Land of the Cumbrians*, pp. 58-61. See also pp. 166, 169 for Ecgfrith and Rheged.

21   Bede, *Vita Cuthberti*, 27, trans. Colgrave.

22   Another possibility, as we will see below, is South Shields: this would have been rather further than Bamburgh from possible Pictish retaliation: perhaps even further than was Carlisle.

23   Bede, *Historia Ecclesiastica*, IV 26.

24   *Annals of Ulster*, s.a. 687 (=686).

25   Symeon of Durham, *Libellus de exordio atque procursu istius hoc est Dunhelmensis Ecclesie*, I 9, ed. D.W. Rollason, (Oxford, 2000), p. 47, with note 59. For Ecgfrith's family links with the Pictish king Brude, see Plummer, *Baedae Opera Historica*, II, p. 261.

26   *Annals of Ulster*, 687 (=686).

27   Charles-Edwards, *Early Christian Ireland*, p. 341.

28   Bede, *Historia Ecclesiastica*, IV 18, 26.

29   For Jarrow as a royal foundation, Wood, *The Most Holy Abbot Ceolfrid*, pp. 2-5.

30   *Vita Ceolfridi*, 11: Bede, *Historia Abbatum*, 7, 15.

31   *Vita Ceolfridi*, 12: Bede, *Historia Abbatum*, 9.

32   Bede, *Historia Abbatum*, 6.

33   *Vita Ceolfridi*, 8: his initial transfer to Wearmouth may not have been voluntary: in *Vita Ceolfridi*, 5 he is sent by Wilfrid.

34   *Vita Ceolfridi*, 11, 25: Bede, *Historia Abbatum*, 7, 13.

35   *Vita Ceolfridi*, 11.

36   Bede, *Historia Abbatum*, 11.

37   *Vita Ceolfridi*, 7.

38   *Vita Ceolfridi*, 13.

39   *Vita Ceolfridi*, 14.

40   For the arguments on either side, Wood, *The Most Holy Abbot Ceolfrid*, p. 34.

41   John of Worcester, *Chronicle*, s.a. 685, ed. R.R. Darlington and P. McGurk (Oxford, 1995), pp. 142-3.

42   Plummer, *Baedae Opera Historia* (Oxford, 1896), II, p. 362.

43   Bede, *Historia Abbatum*, 9.

44   Bede, *Historia Abbatum*, 15.

45   *Vita Ceolfridi*, 16. The privilege in question must be that of pope Agatho for Wearmouth: Bede, *Historia Abbatum*, 6. It was confirmed immediately by Ecgfrith.

46   This second privilege was secured from pope Sergius, and confirmed by Aldfrith: Bede, *Historia Abbatum*, 15. A case for it being explicitly for Jarrow can be deduced from the fact that the surrounding sentences in Bede's account seem to be concerned with St Paul's. If so, this is a

further indication of a distinction between the two houses. Plummer, *Baedae Opera Historica*, II, p. 360, seems unaccountably to get the two privileges confused.

47   *Vita Ceolfridi*, 19.

48   Bede, *Historia Abbatum*, 13.

49   *Vita Ceolfridi*, 25.

50   Bede, *Historia Abbatum*, 11.

51   Bede, *Historia Abbatum*, 8.

52   Bede, *Historia Abbatum*, 13.

53   *Vita Ceolfridi*, 11: Bede, *Historia Abbatum*, 4, 7.

54   Bede, *Historia Abbatum*, 15.

55   Bede, *Historia Abbatum*, 15.

56   *Historia de sancto Cuthberto*, 26, ed. T.J. South (Woodbridge, 2002).

57   *Vita Ceolfridi*, 23.

58   *Vita Ceolfridi*, 25.

59   *Vita Ceolfridi*, 29: Bede, *Historia Abbatum*, 18.

60   *Vita Ceolfridi*, 30: Bede, *Historia Abbatum*, 19.

61   Alcuin, ep. 282, ed. E. Dümmler, *Monumenta Germaniae Historica, Epistolae* IV = *Karolini Aevi* II (Berlin, 1895).

62   Alcuin, ep. 19.

63   Alcuin, ep. 286.

64   Alcuin, ep. 284.

65   Plummer, *Baedae Opera Historica*, I, p. xi, n. 2.

66   See M.S. Parker, 'An Anglo-Saxon monastery in the lower Don valley', *Northern History* 21 (1985), pp. 19-32.

67   Symeon of Durham, *Libellus de exordio atque procursu istius hoc est Dunhelmensis Ecclesie*, II 5, ed. Rollason, p. 89.

68   Rollason, *Symeon, Libellus de exordio*, pp. xlviii-ix.

69   *Historia Regum*, s.a. 794, ed. T. Arnold, *Symeon of Durham*, Rolls Series 75, 2 (London, 1885): he was probably using a Northumbrian chronicle compiled in York: P. Hunter-Blair, 'Observations on the Historia Regum attributed to Symeon of Durham', in N.K. Chadwick, ed., *Celt and Saxon* (Cambridge, 1963), pp. 98-9, reprinted in Hunter-Blair, Anglo-Saxon Northumbria. C. Hart, 'Byrhtferth's Northumbrian Chronicle', *English Historical Review* 97 (1982), pp. 558-82, at p. 560 for the *Historia Regum*, and at pp. 562-3 for an account of the material covering the years 732-802.

70   Ed. W. Stubbs, *Rolls Series* 51 (London, 1868): Parker, 'An Anglo-Saxon monastery in the lower Don valley', p. 20: for the *Historia post Bedam* preserved by Roger, Hart, 'Byrhtferth's Northumbrian Chronicle', p. 560, with n. 3.

71   The material is all conveniently gathered in Parker, 'An Anglo-Saxon monastery in the lower Don valley', p. 20: for Henry of Huntingdon's dependence on the same *Historia post Bedam* used by Roger of Howden, Hart, 'Byrhtferth's Northumbrian Chronicle', p. 560, n. 3.

72   Parker, 'An Anglo-Saxon monastery in the lower Don valley', p. 25.

73   Parker, 'An Anglo-Saxon monastery in the lower Don valley': W. Richardson, 'The Venerable Bede and a lost Saxon monastery in Yorkshire', *Yorkshire Archeological Journal* 57 (1985), pp. 15-22.

74   Bede, *Historia Ecclesiastica*, IV 21-2. In general on these issues, P. Hunter-Blair, 'The Northumbrians and their southern frontier', *Archaeologia Aeliana*, 4th ser., 26 (1948), p. 103, reprinted in id., *Anglo-Saxon Northumbria* (London, 1984).

75   Parker, 'An Anglo-Saxon monastery in the lower Don valley', p. 25.

76   Paul I, ep. to Eadberht, A.W. Haddan and W. Stubbs, *Councils and Ecclesiastical Documents relating to Great Britain and Ireland*, vol. III (Oxford, 1879), pp. 394-6.

77   Parker, 'An Anglo-Saxon monastery in the lower Don valley', pp. 22-3.

78   Alcuin, *Versus de patribus, regibus et sanctis Euboricensis Ecclesiae*, l. 1294, ed. P. Godman, Alcuin: *The Bishops, Kings and Saints of York* (Oxford, 1983).

79   Alcuin, ep. 284. Bede is mentioned also in ep. 19 to Wearmouth and Jarrow, but there is no mention of him in ep. 286 to Jarrow, or in ep. 282 to abbot Friduin of Wearmouth/Jarrow.

80   Bede, *Historia Ecclesiastica*, V 21, 24.

81   Alcuin, *Versus*, l. 1294: epp. 19, 286.

82   Since Eadbert was the brother of Bishop Ecgbert of York, to whom Bede addressed his famous letter on pastoral care and the need for monastic reform, one wonders whether his seizure of the three monasteries should be understood in a positive light.

83   Richardson, 'The Venerable Bede and a lost Saxon monastery in Yorkshire', p. 20, referring to D. Whitelock, trans., *The Anglo-Saxon Chronicle* (London, 1961), p. 37, n. 1. The Latin is to be found in A.W. Haddan and W. Stubbs, ed., *Councils and Ecclesiastical Documents relating to Great Britain and Ireland*, vol. 3, *The English Church* 595-1066 (Oxford, 1871), pp. 394-6. It is not clear from the Latin whether Æthelwold was the brother of the abbess, or of abbot Forthred: the *eius* ought to refer to the former, but one cannot be sure that the author has correctly used *eius* rather than *suo*. For Æthelwold to have been the brother of Eadbert a *tuo* would be required.

84   Bede, *Historia Abbatum*, 11.

85   Boniface, ep. 76, ed. M. Tangl, *Die Briefe des Heiligen Bonifatius und Lullus, Epistolae Selectae* I (Berlin, 1916).

86   Lull to Cuthbert = Boniface, ep. 116: also 127.

87   On Stonegrave and Coxwold, see Wood, 'Monasteries and the geography of power'.

88   Bede, *Vita Cuthberti*, 3, trans. Colgrave. The discussion of the passage by S. Foot, *Veiled Women*, vol. I (Aldershot, 2000), p. 52, unaccountably raises the old misrepresentation of Bede's account, placing the nunnery on the north bank of the Tyne.

89   Colgrave, *Two Lives of Saint Cuthbert*, pp. 342-3 has a discussion of the place involved, and revives the suggestion that this monastery south of the Tyne was also the first monastery entered by Hild: Bede, *Historia Ecclesiastica*, IV 23. This is frankly a red herring: Hild entered a monastery 'ad septentionalem plagam Uiuri fluminis': to describe a monastery on the south bank of the Tyne as being on the north bank of the Wear is absurd. If anything the house which Hild entered should be looked for in the region of Wearmouth: it may even have been a precursor on the same site: she entered the nunnery before the death of Aidan in 651, more than twenty years before the establishment of Biscop's monastery.

90   Bede, *Vita Cuthberti*, 35, 37. In c. 35 he says that he has already mentioned the monastery, which must be a reference back to c. 3. On Verca, see also S. Foot, *Monastic Life in Anglo-Saxon England* (Cambridge, 2006), pp. 216, 236.

91   P. Bidwell and S. Speak, *Excavations at South Shields Roman Fort*, vol. I (Newcastle-upon-Tyne, 1994), pp. 45-6.

92   The seventh- to ninth-century finds so far identified consist of a very fine gilded mount in copper alloy, copper-alloy and bone pins, a pin beater, stylus and two gaming pieces.' Personal communication from Paul Bidwell.

93   J. Leland, *De Rebus Britannicis Collectanea*, ed. altera, ed. T. Hearne, vol. IV (London, 1774), p. 43: 'E regione Tinemutha fuit urbs vastata a Danis Urfa nomine, ubi natus erat Oswinus rex.'

94   Bidwell and Speak, *Excavations at South Shields Roman Fort*, I, p. 42. A. Breeze, 'The British-Latin place-names, *Arbeia, Corstopitum, Dictim*, and *Morbium*', *Durham Archaeological Journal* 16 (2001), p. 21, proposes that the original British name was derived from *Erfin*, and meant '(place by a) stream of wild turnips'. *Urfa* could easily have been derived from the proposed British *Erfin*. Leland does not appear to have called the place *Caer Urfa*, despite the assertion by Bidwell and Speak.

95   Bidwell and Speak, *Excavations at South Shields Roman Fort*, I, pp. 46-7

96   On his descent, Bede, *Historia Ecclesiastica*, III 14. On other certainly fallacious associations of Oswine with Bernicia see *Historia de Sancto Cuthberto*, 3, ed. South, with commentary on pp. 72-3. On the relations between the Bernicians and Deirans, see now Wood, 'Monasteries and the geography of power'.

97   Bede, *Historia Ecclesiastica*, IV 23.

98   *Vita Oswini Regis*, 4, ed. J. Raine, *Miscellanea Biographica, Publications of the Surtees Society 2* (London, 1838): the evidence is discussed by Plummer, *Baedae Opera Historica*, II, p. 164.

99   *Vita Oswini Regis*. 25-6, with Raine, *Miscellanea Biographica*, pp. vii-viii.

100   Roger of Wendover, *Flores Historiarum*, s.a. 651, ed. H.O. Coxe (London, 1841-4), vol. I, p. 504-5: Matthew Paris, *Chronica Majora*, s.a. 651, ed. H. R. Luard, *Rolls Series* 57 (London, 1872), vol. I, p. 287. Both authors also record the later history of Oswine's relics s.a. 1065.

101   M. Still, *The Abbot and the Rule: Religious Life at St Albans, 1290-1349* (Aldershot, 2002), pp. 147-56.

102   Although the discovery of Oswine's relics is mentioned s.a. 1065 in the *Historia Regum*, in the *Libellus de exordio*, III 7 and IV 4, Symeon of Durham is less forthcoming about them. Perhaps he had his suspicions about their authenticity: H.H.E. Craster, *The Parish of Tynemouth*, = *A History of Northumberland*, vol. VIII (London, 1907), left open the question of whether Oswine really was buried at Tynemouth.

103   Leland, *De Rebus Britannicis Collectanea*, IV, p. 43.

104   W.S. Gibson, *The History of the Monastery of Tynemouth in the diocese of Durham* (London, 1846-7), vol. II, p. 95, n. 2. For the manuscript, see H.O. Coxe, *Catalogus codicum MSS. qui in collegiis aulibusque oxoniensibus hodie adservantur* (Oxford, 1852), pp. 49-50. Plummer, himself a Corpus man, noted the manuscript: *Baedae Opera Historica*, II, p. 162. It is not clear, however, why Gibson identifies this manuscript as the source of the information. The main *vita* of Oswine in the manuscript is the same as that edited by Raine from BL Cotton Julius, A. X for the Surtees Society (see above, n. 88). For another *vita* see *Acta Sanctorum*, August, vol. 4 (= August 20th), pp. 57-66.

105   Leland, *De Rebus Britannicis Collectanea*, IV, p. 43: 'Edwinus, rex Northumbrorum, sacellum erexit Tinemutae ex ligno, in quo Rosella, ejus filia, postea velum sacrum accepit. S. Oswaldus monasteriolum de Tinemuthe ex ligneo lapideum fecit.' For the archaeology of Tynemouth, R.J. Cramp, 'Monastic sites', in D. Wilson, ed., *The Archaeology of Anglo-Saxon England*, paperback edn. (Cambridge, 1986), pp. 217-20.

106   Stephanus, *Vita Wilfridi*, 17.

107   Leland, *De Rebus Britannicis Collectanea*, IV, p. 42.

108   *Liber Vitae Ecclesiae Dunelmensis*, ed. J. Stevenson, *Publications of the Surtees Society* 13 (London, 1841), pp. 1-2.

109   *Anglo-Saxon Chronicle*, MS E, s.a. 792. Could Osred, a king who, like Oswine, was murdered, have been mistaken for the martyr?

110   Compare Sutton Hoo being on the north bank of the Deben, opposite the royal vill of Woodbridge, see I.N. Wood, 'The Franks and Sutton Hoo', in I.N. Wood and N. Lund, ed., *People and Places in Northern Europe 500-1600: Essays in honour of Peter Hayes Sawyer* (Woodbridge, 1991), p. 13.

111   A.L.F. Rivet and C. Smith, *The Place-Names of Roman Britain* (London, 1979), p. 256.

112   Technically, suggestions that the fort was a royal site in the time of Oswine would not be incompatible with it being a monastery shortly thereafter. Oswiu's votive foundations following Penda's death could provide a context: Bede, *Historia Ecclesiastica*, III 24. Tynemouth, where Oswine was buried, across the water, would have been an appropriate neighbour. Equally, identification of *Donemutha* with *Arbeia* would mean that the destruction by the Vikings noted by Leland could be identified as the 794 raid on *Donemutha* in Symeon of Durham. Nevertheless, I prefer to see *Donemutha* as lying outside *Urfa*.

113   For Symeon, see above: for Roger of Howden, see Hart, 'Byrhtferth's Northumbrian Chronicle', p. 560.

114   See Parker, 'An Anglo-Saxon monastery in the Lower Don Valley', p. 20: Henry of Huntingdon, however, seems to have had access to the same northern material: Hart, 'Byrhtferth's Northumbrian Chronicle', p. 560, n. 3.

115   *Anglo-Saxon Chronicle*, MS E, s.a. 794.

116   Symeon, *Libellus de exordio*, II 5.

117   *Anglo-Saxon Chronicle*, MS E, s.a. 794.

118   D. Stocker and P. Everson, 'The Straight and Narrow Way: Fenland Causeways and the Conversion of the Landscape in the Witham Valley, Lincolnshire', in M. Carver, ed., *The Cross Goes North: Processes of Conversion in Northern Europe, AD300-1300* (Woodbridge, 2003), pp. 271-88.

119   Leland, *De Rebus Britannicis Collectanea*, IV, p. 43: Bidwell and Speak, *Excavations at South Shields Roman Fort*, I, pp. 46-7.

120   Comparable density is, however, to be found in the Vale of Pickering: see Wood, 'Monasteries and the geography of power'.

121   Bede, *Vita Cuthberti*, 3.

122   Bede, *Vita Cuthberti*, 3.

123   Foot, *Veiled Women*, I, pp. 52-3.

124   *Vita Ceolfridi*, 11.

125   Bede, *Vita Cuthberti*, 27, 28. Foot, *Veiled Women*, I, p. 42, assumes that she became a nun at her sister's monastery in Carlisle, although this is not actually stated.

126   Stephanus, *Vita Wilfridi*, 24, 34, 39, 40.

127   Stephanus, *Vita Wilfridi*, 17, calls Ecgfrith 'rex Christianissimus et piissimus'.

128   *Vita Ceolfridi*, 11.

129   Symeon, *Libellus de Exordio*, I 9, ed. Rollason, p. 47, with note 59. For Ecgfrith's family links with the Pictish king Brude, see Plummer, *Baedae Opera Historica*, II, p. 261.

130   *Annals of Ulster*, 687 (=686).

131   Edwin and Oswald are both good examples: Bede, *Historia Ecclesiastica*, II 20, III 12.

132   One might also note the evocative place name Ecgfrith's Place just to the north of Jarrow monastery, to be found on Simon Temple's map of c.1800.

133   J. Haywood, *Dark Age Naval Power* (London, 1991), pp. 61, 75.

134   Bede, *Historia Ecclesiastica*, IV 26.

135   Bede„ *Historia Ecclesiastica*, IV 27.

136   Bede, *Historia Ecclesiastica*, III 11.

137   D.R. Howlett, 'The provenance, date and structure of *De Abbatibus*', *Archaeologia Aeliana*, 5th series, 3 (1975), pp. 121-30.

138   Plummer, *Baedae Opera Historica*, II, p. 164: Leland, *De Rebus Britannicis Collectanea*, IV, p. 42: *Anglo-Saxon Chronicle*, MS E, s.a. 792.

139   The evidence is collected by Foot, Veiled Women, I, p. 72, with n. 46: Roger of Wendover, *Flores Historiarum*, s.a. 1065, vol. I, pp. 504-5: Matthew Paris, *Chronica Majora*, s.a. 1065, vol. I, p. 531: Leland, *De Rebus Britannicis Collectanea*, IV, p. 114.

140   Bede, *Historia Ecclesiastica*, III 6, 12, 16, 17.

141   Bede, *Vita Cuthberti*, 27.

142   Stephanus, *Vita Wilfridi*, 60.

143   See Wood, 'Monasteries and the geography of power'.

144   See, for example, N.J. Higham, *(Re-)Reading Bede: the* Ecclesiastical History *in context* (London, 2006).

145   For a discussion of Bede's understanding of tides, W.M. Stevens, *Bede's Scientific Achievement*, Jarrow Lecture 1985 (Newcastle-upon-Tyne, 1986).